Lightning Strikes Twice

Mari Selby

Of Sticks and Stones
Staunton, Virginia
2013

Poetry Copyright © 2013 by Mari Selby
Artwork Copyright © 2013 by Jennet Inglis

All Rights Reserved

All rights reserved. No part of this book may be reproduced or transmitted in any form or by any means, electronic or mechanical. This includes photocopying or recording by any information storage or retrieval system, without written permission from the publisher.

Of Sticks and Stones
POB 791
Staunton, VA 24402

www.ofsticksandstones.org

ISBN — 978-0-9884470-0-4

Mari Selby — Cover Photograph
Jennet Inglis — Photograph Composition
Mayapriya Long of Bookwrights — Cover Design
Rita Mills — Interior Design & Layout

Printed in the United States of America

Dedication

With all my love to Mother Earth — Gaia

I dedicate Lightning Strikes Twice to
all the women I have met and loved
through several decades.
May these poems inspire you to
live more wildly, love more deeply,
and find an authentic voice to
express your unique and awesome selves.

Table of Contents

Introduction	7
Chapter One — Water	
This is Not How I Thought I Would be Remembered — Part One	13
Rich with Gratitude	15
Faster Than a Mint Julep	17
Grandmother Mirror	19
First Lightning Dreamed Thunder	20
Hot Red Pepper Overalls	21
Aftershocks	22
For Eagle Eyes	23
A Hunger for Freedom	24
Chapter Two — Fire	
Are you A Woman or A Mouse?	27
Bloated	28
Goddess Spawn	29
Kaleidoscope	31
We Are All Stars	33
Cells of Every Woman	36
Medusa's Pride	41

Chapter Three — Air
- This is Not How I Thought I Would be Remembered — Part Two   47
- Mother's Tears   49
- You Don't Need a Weatherman to Know Which Way the Wind Blows   50
- Strong Laughter   51
- Primordial Essence   52
- Crazy Wisdom   55

Chapter Four — Earth
- How Green Does My Garden Grow   59
- Cycles of Grace   61
- Winter Solstice The Crone's Answer   63
- Twelve Steps on a Medicine Wheel   65
- A New Story Emerges   70
- Sticks and Stones   72
- Lightning Strikes Twice   76

Author Bio   79
Artist Bio   81

Introduction

Author's Note

Writing and reading poetry has always been an intrinsic part of my life. From the poets Emily Dickinson, and Robert Frost as a child, to Judy Grahn and Maya Angelou as an adult, poets and their words have always inspired and supported me. I am also a wordsmith who loves the etymology of words, as well as the physicality of using words to paint pictures of what I see and feel. Writing poetry requires a keen eye, an open mind and heart and most importantly a great editor! I am grateful to Nuccia Hardrich, Jennet Inglis, Malene Bell, and other writing coaches for encouraging me, and being tough with me when necessary to craft a poem until it is "just right".

The title was suggested by my muse, Jennet Inglis. Jennet has lived with me for a few decades. She knew that I was struck by lightning (literally) once, metaphorically twice as a cancer survivor, and spiritually as often as needed for my own evolution. For me the title embraces the luck of a survivor, the luck of being able to write a second poetry book, and the luck of the flash of spiritual illumination that occurs when lightning strikes twice!

Each chapter highlights one of the 4 elements; earth, air, water and fire. Dividing up the book into elemental chapters gives you, the reader both context and room to breathe with each section. Chapter One is "Water"; emotional, personal, memories, sensual; and offering an introduction to my background. Chapter Two is "Fire"; wrathful, dynamic, passionate, social; and offering catalysts for change and power. Chapter Three is "Air"; ephemeral, divinely feminine, sky-going, wisdom, offering your souls union with something greater than yourself. Chapter Four is "Earth"; grounded, cyclical, recovering, becoming solid and offering your body fierce grace. Jennet's enchanting engravings portray each of the four elements.

My first book of poems *We Are All Stars* was published in 1975 by Jackrabbit Press, a feminist press in Eugene, Oregon. Since then I have published poems in numerous anthologies and magazines. Most recently my poetry has been published in "Master Heart" magazine.

Decades of poetry and several geographical locations are represented here. For example: "Bloated", "Goddess Spawn", and "Are You a Woman or a Mouse" written in the 1990's, were inspired by my menstrual cycle. "Cycles of Grace" and "Mother's Tears" were written when I lived in Northern New Mexico. "How Green Does My Garden Grow" was written while living in the Shenandoah Valley of Virginia. "Cells of Every Woman" and "Sticks and Stones" were begun in the 1990's, revised several times, and finally finished in 2011.

Today I am an ambitious crone, experienced entrepreneur, cancer survivor and a fierce spiritual warrior. Earthquakes, thunder storms, morning fog, buttercups, and snow angels spark a state of wonder in my heart. Daily I strive to walk the line between laughter and tears, and no hope and no fear. That line I describe as fierce grace.

Lightning Strikes Twice

Water

Chapter One

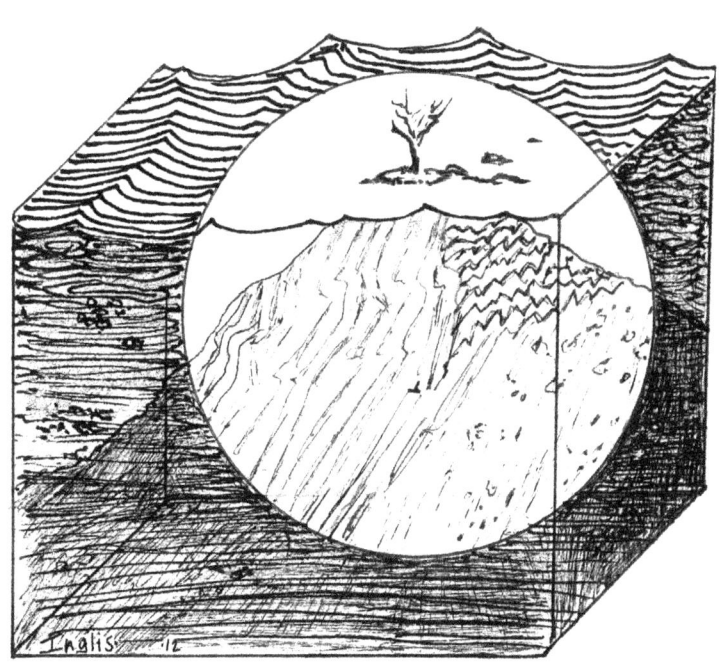

This is Not,
How I Thought I Would be Remembered
Part One

certainly not the little things
rolling of big brown eyes when you say something foolish
mouth open wide to let the laughter roll out
ringlets at the base of the neck
pitter patter of feet walking through leaves
surely not the homely things
posole with green chile and fresh cilantro
turkey tofu meatloaf with steamed broccoli
gingersnap cookies and gluten free chocolate cakes
tomato juice that blasts open taste buds, delivered from the
heirloom tomato plants standing stiff and staked
backyard garden full of Poblano peppers,
Japanese eggplants and the forever encroaching
        Jerusalem artichokes
on your side jungles of zinnias, roses, and dahlias
bouquets of flowers conveyed home when you could not garden
striped socks, and flannel pajamas with kitties on them
bought for holiday and birthday presents
handmade paper and European pastels given as a surprise
definitely little things like the love of two small dogs
sunsets down the street, and out over the mesa
full moons in backyards, and by the Rio Grande
drumming softly at first, then calling all the elemental helpers
laughing at silly songs and roaring wildly like Dakinis

surely the vision was the big things, acts that matter,
courage in saving lives, from burning buildings,

from bloody accidents, or raging rivers
alcoholic stupors or heaters thrown at showers
writing words that blazon across the sky
full of insight and encouragement
inspiring women to create finer lives while
madly publishing books with your artwork across covers
famous for the guidance from the stars
recognized for great kindness, and constant generosity
well-known for supporting the causes of the earth
knowing safety and comfort of abundance
standing by your side as more and more paintings
fly out from your studio, to hang on walls everywhere
definitely to be known for magnificence and giving great joy.

Rich with Gratitude

For my connection to God as I know Her, God who guides me and protects me, God who watches over me and shows me the way towards freedom

For my connection to the majesty of nature, her gifts fly in daily as birds and feathers for my garden, for the transformation of clouds, for the air itself?

For my inspiring lover and friend of 23 years, for my amazing and beautiful lover, for my lover who shows me the way, and takes care of me so well

For my intuition and willingness to listen to God's whisper, God's shout when I am being blockheaded, to God's caress when I can't hear anymore

For the kindness of strangers who have become friends, or with strangers offering kindness when they know so little of me

For the UVA medical system that has prolonged my life, for their knives and needles and the doctors who wield them, for UVA who helped me move beyond pain and depression into being whole and filled with passion

For my move to Virginia where dogs are welcomed everywhere, where people look you in the eye, to Virginia where it doesn't seem to matter who you are as much as how you act

For this small Shenandoah town grateful for my poetry, small town where I wave at friends downtown, small town safe enough to breathe, and blossom

For my body for teaching me to listen, my body for giving me clear signs, my body for recovering, my body carrying me so well for so long?

For my mind for being open to learn, my mind for searching out answers, my mind for loving a challenge, my mind for embracing the expanse of my gratitude

For my heart for facing my fears, my heart for living in courage, my heart for loving deeply, whether in pain or joy

For my soul for coming into this life with a challenging course for me to run, my soul for attracting the love and caring I needed in this life, my soul for helping me reveal my passions, my soul for driving me towards evolution.

Faster Than a Mint Julep

Thank god no one has ever called me pretty,
I am too fast and furious for trivial things.

The first six months of my life I slept in a baby carriage,
rolling through the shifts from room to room
I watched the ceilings as I lay on my back.
Today I never wear hats; they flatten my curly brown hair,
unlike cool slim blondes, who make the art
of wearing hats look pretty and important.

Thank god no one has ever called me pretty,
I am too smart, and don't know how to spout nothing.

In kindergarten I was told I had "nigger lips"
I went home and asked Mom what that meant.
She replied they're just jealous of your "full lips",
I never learned how to smile with only my lips like
thin-lipped blondes who laugh with their mouths closed,
easily turn people's heads with a "that's incredible", or
      "aren't you sweet".

Thank god no one has ever called me pretty,
I am too pushy and unrefined to handle such sweet sugariness.

I had my first period and a near death experience before
      I was eleven,
back from death enraged to be here, I began my love affair
with chocolate, every afternoon I had a date with Oreos,
my plump ass and I never dated many boys in high school

unlike the blonds whose matching sweater sets
rubbed my thighs wrong, made me sweat with shame.

Thank god no one has ever called me pretty,
I am too chubby and fine to be stuck with high school pictures.

When I came out I was called beautiful, awesome
luscious, and asked often, can I kiss you now?
sex was good, and I cut a fine figure for a goddess woman.
Today I live in Virginia and I am still sexy, love my big mouth
that asks too many questions, too impatient to wait for change,
guaranteed to overwhelm any blonde for miles around.

Thank god no one has ever called me pretty,
I am too swift and wrathful to wait for the mint julep to chill.

Now grey sparks and shoots through my curly hair and
there's a red zipper down my middle where my female organs
used to be, while recovering from cancer, and my addictions,
all my sharp edges are exposed, slowly being licked clean
by God's rough tongue like a round green stone
        resting on a river's bed
reminding one of priceless and simple beauty.

Thank god no one has ever called me pretty,
I am too courageous to live without grace and poetry.

Grandmother Mirror

Granite boulder rooted and dense,
ragged ridges to sudden arroyos.

North wind sings of death
caresses my face with peace.

Clear streams bubble, laugh, cry
shape rock, move mountains.

Generous sun shares your heart
crisps my edges clean.

Grandmother
thank you for being, eyes that saw
hands that held, a heart that cared,
you were always there
caressed with peace
bubbling, laughing crying,
my eyes mirror yours, pain comes
when I believe, that you're not there.

To heal I dissolve in rocks,
streams, wind and sun.

I drink clear water memories,
find you in stories and dreams.

First Lightning Dreamed Thunder

Grandmother's voice in my dreams
enlightened me of your arrival,
I interviewed women in tweed jackets,
hugged broad shoulders, none cracked a roll.
Finally with a surrender, a thunder dream;
delivered long arms and star-filled eyes,
you plucked my heart and made me sigh...
Today our muses frequently inspire
my mouth and your hands.
Juicy words, wondrous images
create a colorful reality, after seven years
radiant colors appear tangible as intimacy and joy.
Magenta inspires YES parties, incites prayers to be heard.
Red heals cat fights, through humble revelations of brattiness.
Orange brings lessons of chronic pain, and romps in Abiqui lake.
Yellow connects our bodies to everything under the sun.
Green grows abundance of luscious gardens, and soon money.
Blue flows sudden showers of tears, and silly songs of a child.
Indigo summons our Pleiades kin, and memories of other lives.
Violet sizzles summer lightning, and hot oceanic sex.
Magenta opens the future...a rose will be a rose,
and neither gophers nor mothers
will stop me from being Gertrude, to your Alice
or you from being Gertrude to me.

Hot Red Pepper Overalls

Searching for answers
I saw your heart beat on a black and white screen,
at first my heart hurt
when I was left with still more questions.

Earlier that summer, adventures were the dusty wind
of the flea market,
I saw them
waving insistently HI!
Hot red pepper colored overalls
hung by their straps,
daring me to pass them by.
when I tugged on your sleeve
to watch the overalls dance
a little girl's face that never had and always wanted,
beamed out from your very pale freckled one.
The next morning you decked out
complete with red high tops and white star shirt
a brave and rosy sight,
while you wobbled on your long legs.

Today when I saw your sweet heart beat, I
heard the song of your valves and chambers
and knew this as music full of love and hope for me.

Aftershocks

aftershocks
come crash upon
the shore of my body
wave after wave
of foam
breaks
recedes
the I of myself
lost over the horizon
my body radiates
without thought
after the shocks
fade away
gradually I calm
turn my head
call you bliss
even though
I know that's
not your name

For Eagle Eyes

love flows hot grabs me
rushes up my back
bumps and grinds
to a soulful tune
my ears flood with heat
brushes the top of my head
kisses my face
slides heartward
home, a love song
my soul remembers.

A Hunger for Freedom

rain blesses my head, tears spatter my face,
pain wells up spreads
thick ink blots puzzled over,
puzzle pieces in an ocean of pain.
A lifetime of hunger for freedom,
unfurls the crack of a flag,
when the wind whips through,
a prayer whispered at a shrine
when nothing's to gain or lose.
Tears salty sweet, pain a familiar brew,
I long for a cool drink of my own reflection,
whole shining, for all to see.
Safe my heart searches, through dark nights,
ring out with the sound of courage to dream,
to dream again, of freedom to touch,
be touched, without shadows.
Courage, to give voice to thunder,
and be felt as solid, true as the Earth.

Fire

Chapter Two

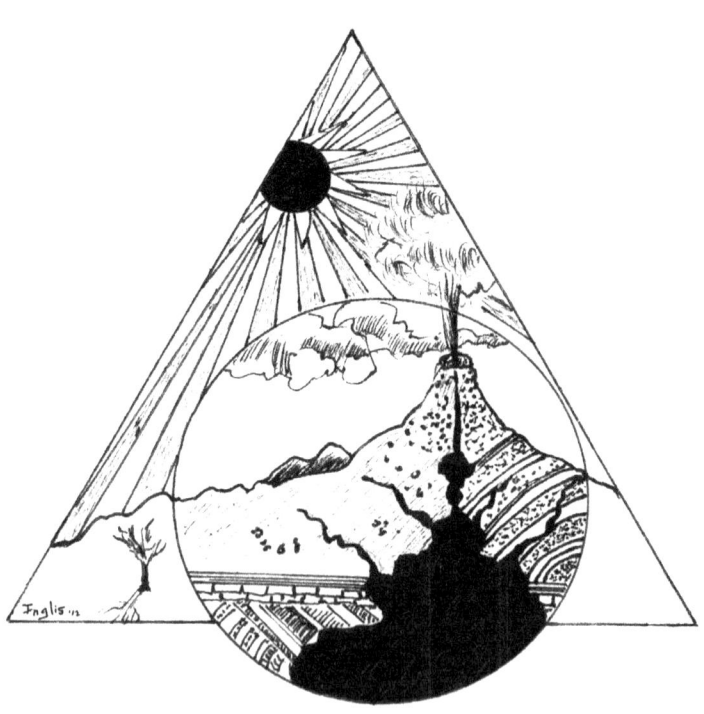

Are You A Woman or A Mouse?

I want to rip faces off,
flay skin from bodies,
ride through the night
whip dreams into nightmares,
echo with screams of rage.
Molten heavy memories
stream off my body,
about to erupt.
Men call me PMS
give me deodorant pads
to catch my bloody mess.
Read these lips
I am not about to bleed
become hysterical
or surrender.
I am tired of doing the expected
Smiling, being soft and nice,
my belly's had enough sweetness.
No plastic plugs toxic shock for me.
Instead, I am raw,
patches of skin rupture.
I rub and crawl
thick black soil
frees my body,
emerges salty and scaly
my heart feeds on shadows,
my tongue tastes the air
fangs ready to strike first and
devour any mouse in my path.

Bloated

Hungrily I pace my calendar hunting for blood,
ready to explode, the moon inches around her course.
I look into the mirror and can't see myself
Maybe I am a plump white fish out of water,
belly swollen with tears, sobs flooding her last breath.
Or maybe, a sly porcupine disguising herself as a red balloon
unaware of the obstacles in her path.
Or maybe the Pre-Murder Special slipping into night's waiting,
a well of witchy rage burns in my womb...
am I a bloated bitch from hell?
Or maybe a fat tigress licking her lips
her sashay growing looser her scent dancing in nostrils
an image of an itch being scratched flickers in her eyes.
my body a time bomb readying to explode
continuing to pace until sighting the first drop
my blood comes again, my body reeking crazy female wisdom
free at last, a seventh sister guides me back home

Goddess Spawn

Slap my thighs
declare my delicious bleedingness
shake with rich laughter, shiver with fierce knowing,
nothing's to lose
old wives tales to digest,
study thick red clots search for fortune
bright bloody specks spurt from my proud womb,
a generous sign of health
Sly ghosts of shame,
the mute mad-woman in the corner,
does not catch me in her web

Chorus: 1 AM A BIG BAD BOLD BEAUTY BLEEDING

Stand my lusty strong legs spread wide
feel the surge, echo, of countless salty seas
flow from my own and numberless women's legs
sharp edged shiny plastic captures
the beautiful "stinking mess".....
baby powder hides the smell of woman
spontaneous sparks ignite
as legs chafe against a man-made universe
        stomp, dance
the earth my partner
legs roar quiver with rage

Chorus: 1 AM A BIG BAD BOLD BEAUTY BLEEDING

Suffer perverse truths
lose my step between moon time
on the rag, the curse
time of the month, period
lost out of control crazy body wisdom lover and guide
seize rags of shame in a mad embrace
ghostly remnants appear as biting cramps
to remind me of the true wisdom of the body
cracks open, my lusty strong legs split
grow longer, blood splatters
everywhere, shamelessly

Chorus: I AM A BIG BAD BOLD BEAUTY BLEEDING

Spin wildly, my body has been spun easily
between mother's daughter,
the Mother's child, and Daddy's girl,
dizzy with karma, shed an old skin ready to
devour niceness, obstacles on my path
cycles of great bliss to reclaim
led by a murmur growing louder
by the light of rage, pride swelling
to birth a wild woman/goddess
for every woman's dreams
a shout...to be cast around the earth

Chorus: I AM A BIG BAD BOLD BEAUTY BLEEDING
I AM A BIG BAD BOLD BEAUTY BLEEDING

Kaleidoscope

Bright pieces of glass form patterns, light reveals their beauty
apricot, lemon yellow slivers slip into place
autumn sunsets golden drinkable ecstasy, afterwards
lavender silhouettes the rooftops of faded houses
a white-haired plump gardening woman wears baggy khakis
tenderly carries a brown basket full with the last of the harvest
Japanese eggplant, Poblano and Banana peppers, green tomatoes
she shuffles slowly inside, her tremors greet her many cats

Maiden, Virgin, Mother, Crone
Kaleidoscope of love springs eternally

Delft blue bits, shards of aqua green change
with a twist of the wrist fresh mandalas shift into place
winter's ghostly sunset sharp with echoes of snow trace
blood red shadows of skyscrapers keep a chain smoking
woman company, black mascara hides her eyes, her thin
black leather jacket & mini-skirt reveal too much, she
shivers while she frantically searches for her next trick
pays the rent, God watches over her babies at home...

Summer, Spring, Autumn, Winter
Kaleidoscope of care shines through a glass darkly

Lime and honey chips of glass reflect a siren call
of hope and renewal, the season twitches into place
spring sunsets full of virgin faith, and new life
lingers for licks of rosy grey usher in the night,
a porch sitting black eyeglass wearing, acned teenager
pushes her nose even farther into her chemistry book

struggles to ignore the shouting and crashing
determines to leave this house as soon as possible

Maiden, Virgin, Mother, Crone
Kaleidoscope of faith bubbles up from fathomless wells

Violet flecks of purple, carmen splinters radiate sensuality
as heat lightning flashes the season shimmers into place
summer's extravagant sunsets penetrate hearts of gardens,
guardians for the newly in-love, tee-shirt rolled up sleeves woman
hair brush cut, face clean and shiny, smiles while she
paces hope curls from her nostrils like smoke and
the weight of the small black velvet box in her pocket
keeps her sneaker shod feet on the ground.

Summer, Spring, Autumn, Winter
Kaleidoscope of love etches new shapes with each twist and turn.

We Are All Stars

Reach into pockets
spill out our secret dreams
Red arroyos sculpt nightmares & daydreams
shapes a dream march for our rights
legislative acceptance,
for some people a perverse ideal...
Big Daddy, please notice us
give us a pat on the head
our begging bowl is out
pass us a law, declare we are family,
the price is too high.

A broken bleeding woman stumbles back to her car
her hair's too short,
she once walked with a swagger...
an emaciated shadow-eyed man lies in bed
his lover watches through the window,
his family blocks the view...
a child's tears and dripping snot
cover his face hopeless,
ripped from his Mother's arms,
woman lover stands behind her...
two men elegant in their many colors,
gentle in manner watch as all their belongings
pile up on the street,
the price is too high.

Too many years of eating pain that's not ours,
she's my friend, he's just my buddy
we can't go home again, I'll lose my job...
the price is too high.
An invisible cloak of silent shame maims us,
a bull's-eye painted on our hearts
splattered by religious fanatics or
worn hiding in a proud underground culture,
our choice to shit out shame,
or swallow pain again...
we are survivors, who dream march for our lives.

Big Daddy please notice us,
give us a pat on the head
we hungrily wait upon your every word...
legislate our right to be ourselves
and die for our country,
your name is President Clinton,
when we fill our heart with Hope from Arkansas
do we hear more than silence and patience...
A decade later we are promised change
a new president who sets new precedence,
we still pay taxes, but cannot marry
Big Daddy we wait upon your word.
Is the price too high?
We are all stars, reaching for a birthright
more than penises, more than clitorises...
we have faces on our very human bodies
weavers, teachers, doctors, lawyers,
Afro-American, Jewish, Native American, Irish, Buddhist,
nurses, soldiers, truck-drivers, police, reporters

sisters, cousins, daughters, mothers, fathers
we are poets, ministers, artists, and wounded healers
in closets and out, we have sex just like you.

The price of silence is too high
we march
dream for our lives
awake we perceive our journey as
a thread of the dream fabric of the night
children of Earth, our Mother,
we love as we dream, march our way
across a star filled sky.

Cells of Every Woman

Earth Mother, older than Tara, or Kali,
    larger than myth, wiser than her daughters.

Sacred stones their flesh holds,
has always held secrets of enchanted times
more ancient than memory.

bone-creaking sacred witch woman
selling her body working woman
faded, bleached-out mother woman

daughters surviving for our lives

Hecate reminds us that bones decay,
have always decayed into precious gems,
provide gardens full of life.

battered but not beaten woman,
nose picking sharp-tongued woman
thriving on the bones of perpetrators woman

we circle around, circle around

Yemaja's tears flow
have always flowed wildly
simply rivers, female rain.

child-carrying woman
multiple orgasm woman
surviving breast cancer woman

daughters surviving for our lives

Eskagiel's descent into darkness means,
has always meant frightening blizzards
rough glaciers scouring the earth's body.

cave-living holy hermit woman
hard-fisted flint-eyed woman
dark-veiled mourning woman

as we dance, we circle around

Demeter's return celebrates,
has always celebrated apple blossoms
new-born kids and seeds planted with hope.

dreamy flower power woman
raging roaring fat woman
innocent virgin child woman

Earth Mother older than beliefs,
      larger than Jesus, wiser than faith.

Sangre de Cristo Mountains veins,
have always bled with silver,
uranium, treasures of lost ages.

green thumb-nature woman
on the rag, bleeding woman
snake-hearted green-eyed woman

circle around, circle around
Primordial essence blood runs,
has always run as seeds of life slide down,
purification for everywoman.

fat blissful nun woman
matronly soft-bodied wise woman
spitting anxiety-ridden nail-biting woman

daughters struggling for our lives

the earth's sweat feeds,
has always fed thirsty aspen forests,
and dusty gardens with morning dew.

do anything for love woman
mirror-hating anorexic woman
hard-hearted weary nurse woman

daughters struggling for our lives

Everywoman's love erupts
has always erupted from juicy vulvas
between curvaceous hills of lava hips.

luscious muff-diving woman
brassy playboy bunny woman
loud rock and roll woman

as we dance, we circle around

Earth Mother older than war,
    larger than legends, wiser than mountains

Mother nature's rage splinters,
has always splintered night sky
with forks of pink lightening.
flying harpy bitch woman
lightning fast crone woman
middle-class nice woman

daughters struggling for our lives

Allegheny Mountain ribs rise,
have always risen, fallen to the beat
of volcanoes, roll of earthquakes.

raw tired teaching woman
brave mountain-climbing woman
healing hands and hearts woman

we circle around, circle around

Mother Nature's pulse echoes,
has always echoed, in every belly
where life forms, in every whale song

flute-playing seeker woman
sweet country horse woman
white-haired cat loving woman

daughters striving for our lives

Millennia of women's feet drum,
have always drummed a timeless rhythm
felt in every woman's heart.

earthy easy drunk woman
heart-wrenching singing woman
business-minded career woman

daughters striving for our lives

Snake mother, Corn Mother, Star Mother
       idols, altars dance, have always danced in caves.

dreams, cells of every woman.
belly-shaking laughing woman
visionary artist woman
lover of all sentient beings woman

as we dance, we circle around

Earth mother, older than the moon,
       wiser than the sun, larger than life,
       dancing in our every breath.

Medusa's Pride

Mirrors are tricky things
Monday their polished surface
caressed my face with two soft hands
Wednesday I gazed at an empty reflection.
Today must be special, the mirror
grabs me by the throat
forces my nose up against the cool metal
demands I see.
Medusa stares back at me
her wild golden brown pain-filled eyes
hypnotize me, I fall deep
into a murky soup of despair
try to pull away
her snakes clamp on my face.

Medusa your anguish,
over a myth made into a lie
underlines women's oppression
can't be mine, I'm brave,
I only pretend to be.
I see suffering flow into brick walls,
rutted into gravely roads
or burst with hisses of indrawn breath,
shortened by purple bruises from someone's fist.
Your lion face terrifies and agitates,
turns even the strongest birthing mother to stone.

Medusa your merciless eyes a simple mirror,
your myth shouts of betrayal and defeat.

And yet you live,
as stone splinters in everywoman's heart
in black depression, ragged, many-layered,
in chronic biting fiery lower back pain,
in each ripped out breast sacrificed to cancer,
in every savage battle with
en-do-me-tri-o-sis.

Medusa you live on in
survivors managing life with their
tight-lipped smiles hiding clenched teeth;
proud lesbian shoulders
right one bracing against shame
left one down welcoming your strength.
I am surviving
my scars reflect your glory, right eye
torn in battle with forceps at birth,
red zipper from belly button down
still leaves me a woman

Medusa I watch
the fear of your reflection
etch worry frowns into wrinkles,
turn stomachs into ulcers,
appear in winces and flinches,
I catch in other's eyes
dart and dash attempting a puny veil
to block your message,

I am here now, I am woman
faintly at first then stronger
I hear roaring, we are here now,
we are women, your lion's pride come alive

Medusa today must be special,
there you are again
I step away from the mirror
cock my head, flex feisty supple shoulders
lift my hands to frame my ancient face,
with soft quick strokes, I calm the dancing snakes
turn to admire fangs exceedingly sharp
grin at my vital image
graced by your pride,
now gazing back at me.

Air

Chapter Three

This is Not How I Thought I Would be Remembered

Part Two

for facing Cancer twice in 6 years
for staggering through the valley of knives and needles
for limping stiffly with impossible pain
for bearing weak lungs that draw bronchitis like a sponge
for feeling like an invalid too many times
for wearing a red zipper down the middle of the torso
for displaying scars that wrap around the neck
for carrying scars that etch the shoulder, the belly, the eye
for losing sex appeal along with female organs
for gaining weight while battling depression
for gaining more weight like there was no tomorrow
for change comes not through my will, and yet I am willing
for courage does not always roar, sometimes it's a whisper
and change materializes bearing experience, strength and hope

certainly there is hope for climbing of foreign mountains
and exploring of ancient temples,
surely faith will reward dreams of
wonder at the beauty stashed in museums
taste of exotic foods as daily bread for locals,
definitely trust brings the touch of lips, soft and passionate kisses,
create a dance watched over by the heavens,
hold hands while diving into the bluest sea,
positively recovery promises

flight to all the locations on well fingered lists to
nourish hearts while listening to chants,
transport souls to memory of oneness
for surely life is made up of more than little things
elements from supernovas race across universes
become mountains, oceans and rivers,
bodies, hopes, and dreams
for clearly there are angels, and these angels
always lead and sometimes carry through the dark tunnels
oh! great mystery of where there is no hope or fear
and a holograph is greater than the whole
let there be all of me
let me be remembered as this
a shooting star dancing lightly past the moon.

Mother's Tears

I am one and many
we sharply etch out a solo existence
as one we rush together in awful frenzy
as many we merge a quicksilver surrender
as one we emanate a silent inborn rhythm
as many we dare to wash the sun

raindrops breathe and crystallize rainbows
hold colors deep within their heart,
display treasures of lacy prisms of light,
blue sky drops fluffy feathers morph into
liquid limbs tumble lustfully, pirouette and roll
crowd and mob into black blankets of cloud
their fusion ignites outrageous forks,
wiley thunder tickles earth, cracks with laughter
splits arroyos gullies with rushing fingers of water
grow stronger, shape fists, pound brittle leaves, crusty soil,
worn out lonely corn stalks, force adobe walls to surrender,
singing drum of heavy rain, splashes back as tears of life

I am one and many
we roll down ravines
caress serpentine river rocks and Indian Paintbrush
bite down in dusty earth with a lemon awareness
watery fingers lightly rub each fragment of sandy soil
cat tongue the hillsides
laugh with the Tigerlilys as they sway to a dance of
I am one and many

You Don't Need a Weatherman to Know Which Way the Wind Blows

Slim fingers of rain dance miles above
the high desert where great cumulous clouds gather
then disappear over mountains spines,
instead of summer monsoons daily deluge
female rain shimmies over the earth to tease us.
On the mesas, casinos cities of gold, mine hard earned
sweat off hardworking backs and a child's tears,
TV weathermen and preachers
offer slick prayers and stalk for the emptiness in our souls.
Coyotes panting tongues hang down
while cottonwoods throw their arms open in hope
and lettuce leaves ache for a drop of deliverance.
Just when we expect our souls to shrivel up
turn brown like the Pinon trees
magenta sunset hangs in front of our eyes
dancing neutrinos billow across the sky
awaken our reptilian brain, invite us to leave false Gods behind.
Rainbow neutrino spheres activate a living library
our bodies remember how to shape shift,
become frogs and call down the rain,
bulbous throats ululate with ancient vibrations
rain drops fall on upturned faces
parched and thirsty for a change in the weather.

Strong Laughter

Dakini
I am
sky dancing again
right leg raised left leg extended
in the dancing posture
laughing with unbearable bliss,
sweat drips between my breasts, as I
embody a pregnant and celestial mandala
center of the galaxy opens wider as a
cosmic cervix dilates even wider
to birth myself as an ageless innocent
sky dancing again
Dakini
I am

Primordial Essence

One

Skygoer — Dakini come dance with me.
I offer my heart surrender sight smell sound taste touch
to your primordial essence.
A worldly Dakini I walk this Earth body
with rage pain fear my awful companions,
joy peace compassion lotus buds to grow into.
I am all elements, essence of reality
spinning through turn's cycles of joy, bliss life.
Skygoer come dance with me.
In one turn I am changing woman
shooting for the Pleiades,
aiming for a rainbow body.

Dakini come dance with me.
In one turn I travel
an endless road of Samsara
suffering my own creation.

Two

Skygoer — Dakini come dance with me.
I take refuge in you for my life for enlightenment
for all sentient beings.
I offer my heart surrender sight smell sound taste touch
to your protection.
In the mirror of my heart I am terrifying wrathful
a hungry ghost in search for the way out.
My body mandala spinning through cycles lives,
growing in rainbow light.
Skygoer come dance with me.
In one turn I am a great pinwheel
laughing wildly at myself
fireworks of joy bliss freedom my colors.

Dakini come dance with me.
In one turn I am woman
bristling with pain fear rage
begging for release, bleeding
screaming my life away.

Three

Skygoer — Dakini come dance with me.
I offer you my rage pain fear
all that separates, may you feed long well.
I offer you my joy, love, in wonder
may you know primordial bliss.
I vow to hold your ferocity close
compassion my guide, and walk at the edge of my capacity.
I offer you my arms legs hands heart head and body
that I may live in your image.
Skygoer come dance with me.
In each moment I choose myself, a Great spiral wheel
dance of being, dance of light.

Dakini come dance...
In each moment I thank
the Dakini inside
knowing all sentient beings become illuminated.

Skygoer — Dakini come dance with me.

Crazy Wisdom

curling up against Night's belly her tits dust my face
ebony flour gritty with stars
gulping the welcome velvet from the in-between spaces
I find snake belly protection
suffering bondage of self I suck down my heart
through quick gasps of breath
pulling back until my womb aches with lost breaths
        I shudder in climax
become the wet clay of mirror-like mind treasures
generating the primordial source I unroll myself expand
        to inspire an earthy pot,
groping wantonly for an immortal heartbeat
my lips, poise ready to nurse at Night's breast
feed on threads of warmth unravel a thread I am
emptiness full of moment

gaining on my threshold I stumble on my own surrender
soar clumsily into night's heart
penetrates my body the infinite colors of darkness
pierces my heart manifests spikes of light
shuddering at the hot fingers of home
my windy mind ebbs forward wallows in the backwash
melting together as the spices of night bewitch my body
envelop ours in a salty sweet aroma
trembling notes of rapture tumble from juicy lips
we stream beyond a field of dreams
splitting into a thousand pieces of night I lose my self
become diamond mind great space

curling up against night's belly
her velvet cape peopled with stars wraps up my body

dreaming the primordial word
I nestle in the palm of night's hand visible yet empty
blinking in the radiance of the galactic eye
embracing whole worlds of the eye within the eye
perching on my shoulder angels sing hallelujah
invisible paws padding by my feet whisper put faith in every pace
smelling restless noise the tip of my tail twitches I lick my lips
don't stop me before I am lost
curling up against night's belly her great head turns towards me
her gaze stars full of mercy and magic
accepting timeless wonder my breath embraces dakinis devas
the dry rattle of skulls following every movement
praising the diamond night
I am the crazy wisdom of no hope and no fear

Earth

Chapter Four

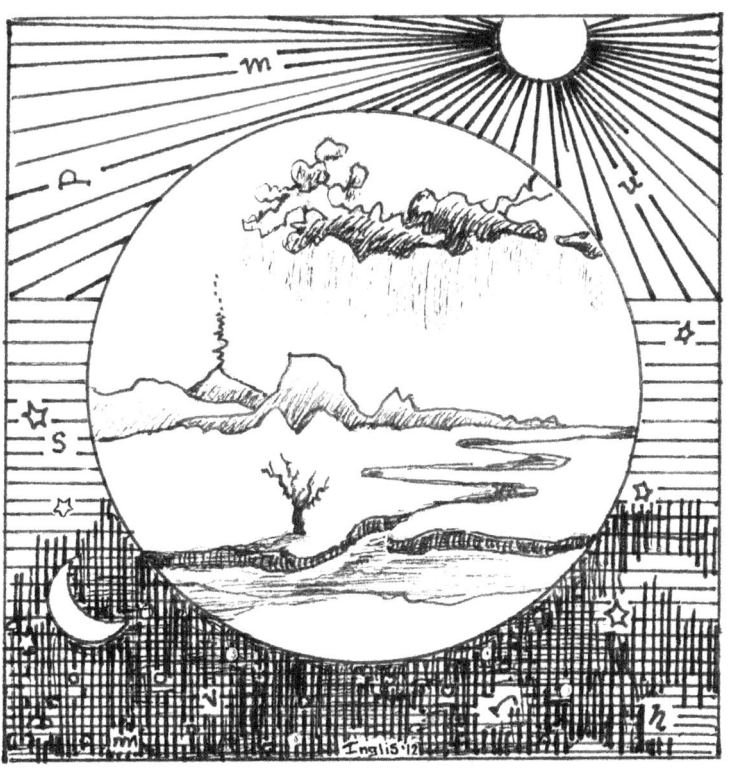

How Green Does My Garden Grow

Out of a dry purple bean a plant spirals
appear freshly green full of showy promise
fills out and becomes a frilly bush
flowers and grows a succulent tender bean

I walk in emptiness a space to call my own
a wide world between my birth and death
echoes with the Mother's whisper
listen and you will blossom
why else are you here but to become that bean?
I shake with fear and still walk onward

Out of a seed, a stalk pushes upwards
straight and strong, from birth
follows the light every inch across the sky
becomes a flower that encompasses the sun

I walk in emptiness a life to call my own
an eternity between my birth and death
echoes with the Mother's tongue
give me your fear, anger and hunger
I dream up compost from these illusions
awaken a concert of green for my garden

Out of mounds of dark earth a garden grows
there squash blossoms glow in early morning light
tomato starts grow inches overnight
tiny pepper plants insist upon producing fruit

I walk in emptiness a time to call my own
a great mystery, between my birth and death
my body creates Cancer again; while my brain needs to know why
the unknown beckons with an open palm,
surrender, yield, and let the mind become a great canyon
echo the Mother's shout to a whisper,

How green does my garden grow?

Cycles of Grace

autumn's light calls my name,
awakens me from summer's slumber
whispers about winter
emanate from sunsets bloated belly.
voluptuous tendrils of molten light
snakes through upper limbs of elm trees,
snags my mind at harvest time when the cycle of death
excites a primordial nature
to embody north wind's first bite,
dance wildly amidst falls quarrelsome leaves
while I devour the golden light.
my outstretched hands embrace,
blend in one fluid motion with the light of sunset
opens my mouth frees my throat
light the color of new honey dribbles on my tongue
round balls roll around
syrupy in my mouth
sucks, on the sweetness of light
first my face, then throat gleam,
the light swallows me.
I am all colors on sunset's palette,
amber catches on shedding willow leaves
breaks up light into puzzle pieces
pink salmon remnants of last season's alfalfa crop,
topaz heaps of fallen leaves,
bleached yellow corn stalks shake like tambourines
jingle echoes and bounces from Jemez Peaks
back to ragged beards of periwinkle snow filled clouds,

caress steel gray bark of cottonwood crowns
shiver in rapture with a final golden lick of light
together we slip,
into a satiated embrace of the long night.

winter junco weaves a quick tune
to warm my frost-nipped ears
reminds me to keep dancing,
clap glove covered fingertips together to applaud
the citrine edge of winter's gaunt sunset
leaches away with watery blood tinged light,
scrapes me clean to my marrow,
purified I call out,
light oh light of spring sunset
cycle through again as a song of hope
return with eternal grace
let me hear you call
my name again.

Winter Solstice—The Crone's Answer

Long cold nights hardly give me enough rest;
you keep calling on me in this my favorite season,
it's my time to dream,
curl up inside my soul while waiting on the light's return

you keep calling,
demanding I get out of my warm bed,
to give you a break from my wintry blasts
that herald a healthier spring,
to fill your emptiness, which you believe hidden from me,
to heal you from flu and chills when purification is necessary.

Now, you have my full and awful attention,
I stand up, my aching knees,
joints cracking in protest
shake out my long graying locks,
look you in the eye,
what is it you really want?

By your constant calling on me,
you have made it plain,
that you want something other than what's given,
before I shower you with abundance as you request,
maybe it's time to take out the garbage,
prepare for a new year?

Wait what presents will you give me?
Gold-plated expectations, or moldy limiting beliefs,
poisonous patterns, or self-will run riot,

or the grace of true gratitude for this experience,
whatever it is, I'll take it all, make it into rich compost
fold it back into my body,
transform it all into nutrients
along with the returning light I will grow young again,
with a promise of a turning of the season I give you
awe and wonder, with a bouquet of joy thrown in,
What will you dream up with these gifts?

Meanwhile I am the brightly colored sweater wrapped around you,
the old radiator that emanates kindness, the cup of ginger tea,
the loving arms of friends and shared conversation,
together we shape winter's tempests like a potter with clay,
   we glaze short days with bright reds and greens,
   we fire dreams in the kiln of the long winter night.

Twelve Steps on a Medicine Wheel

Being held in Creator's hands, my breath came as long sweet sips of life. I face the wheel grandmothers all my relations, I offer up myself tobacco upon wind, corn meal to earth. I am the wheel I walk, in union with spirit I create myself. I watch myself dance the twelve steps, one step at a time.

I am the wheel, the wheel turns

My breath is powerful, with the slightest puff I lace the cottonwoods, etch the mountain peaks with ice. Snow geese flee south my blustery breath pushes against their backs. I blow up clouds until swollen and heavy with waiting they drift into place, release sparks sharp white and cold. These sparks make blankets of white, muffle the mesas, and people retreat inside. My light is crisp whispers sleep, time for long dreams. I blow harder, rattle the icicles that hang from adobe roofs, freeze all in dreamtime. With wind, ice snow my allies renewal and purification take place. I am a crone, Kali, and I come from the north.

Wheel turns

As I run from the cold, darkness falls quickly and demons nip at my heels. I shiver and huddle in the corner where everything must be wrong, and I am not good enough. Life falls heavy on my shoulders, a weight I believe I must carry alone. I check my lists of bruises, and lacerations my companions in dark nights of the soul. Blue and green Pendleton blankets, fire places, and thick books become my best friends, help me to forget. Then memories once again beckon as the shadows deepen, drive me to my knees, to surrender to my first step, my life has become unmanageable. I am a survivor taking one step at a time.

The wheel turns

Kneeling in Creator's hands, my breath loose and deep I am safe, safe here in my center. A power greater than I cradles me in the heart of my world. I turn over, my life love to Creator. I am the night sky spinning on a spiral wheel, a prayer flag whispering in the wind, a crystal full of knowing.

I am the wheel, the wheel turns

I am soft green light breathing apricot branches into buds with a delicate touch. The next minute I can roar, tumble down arroyos to wake up cottonwoods, blowing hard I shout I am here! A blanket of fresh new air warms valleys and garden plots unfold from long dreams, their hearts opening. Rabbits spring from their burrows, and calves are being licked into life. I lavish a tender wash over bean sprouts; I touch lilacs and eagles equally with a rough scrubbing of rain, waking every face I see. My allies wind, rain, and gentle sun bring wisdom and illumination to life. I am a maiden, Quan Yin, and come from the east.

Wheel turns

Ripping plastic off my windows, I once again refuse to see the gathering snow clouds, my will is so strong to make it Spring. While my mind holds onto my long dreams as an opiate I brace my hands to keep the fresh green light of the unknown at bay. I'd rather not know lilacs and tulips; I'm not ready to blossom, my mind is satisfied with the windy places already known. My heart still frozen with fear, shadow fills me with half-truths I can call reality. Light creeps softly every day staying a little longer, asks me to fearlessly look into the shadows within, inventory my past since I cannot control the future.

The wheel turns

Rocked tenderly my sobs subside as I relax, an emotional lodestone returning to magnetic north, knowing I am the wheel, Spirit inside. I am ready to admit my shame and shortcomings to creator and another, willing to turn over my defects. I grow in radiance, a safe humble hearth opening to a loving embrace.

I am the wheel, the wheel turns

My hot breath is sharp and focused; still I nourish all green plants with my strong bright rays. My hard fingers of light stretch into all the rock crevices, lizards and rattlesnakes sunbathe in my dreamtime. My countenance is open; I can wither a squash plant with my gaze, or laugh at corn tassels who dare to hide what grows inside. Pink heat lightening cracks dances at my command, while thick dark clouds burst as a summer blessing, and flash floods wipe the smile off Coyote's face as payback for her mocking my fertility. Thunderstorms are my allies, this hot season I learn trust. I am mother, Tara, I come from the south.

Wheel turns

Sweat drips down my forehead as I struggle with my garden, overgrown with resentment and fear. My back burns in the heat, my arms fight with the grassy weeds. I lift my head up, hold my empty hands out, watch love sift sand through my fingers;

wonder if I expect too much. Sunlight sears the inside of my eyes as tears of rage hang heavy around my face. Coyote nips at my heels demanding I look into the bright light of my desires, to touch and be touched without pain. Thunderstorms name all those I've harmed, and rainbows encourage me to make amends.

The wheel turns

Resting in Creator's embrace, grief flows balm for my wounds; I am safe in my center. Being nurtured I make amends let forgiveness be my medicine. I am a child again, friends with the shadows, willing to admit when I am wrong. Step by step I walk with the Creator, a deep crystalline lake searching for my reflection.

I am the wheel, the wheel turns

I gather sunlight up at the edges of day, wash golden light through the cooling air, dare people to harvest gardens quickly. With a brisk touch of my breath aspen leaves turn yellow, poison oak red, empty corn stalks shimmer and dance. Take my essence to aide in reflection, look in clear waters before leaves blanket mountain lakes and lazy Fall rivers. Bear hungrily stuffs berries and grubs in her large mouth, and Raven's shadow warns of a long sleep coming. Silty river bottoms, golden sunsets are my allies, with experience, introspection builds strength. I am matron, Yemaja, I come from the west.

Wheel turns

In my headlong rush away from harvesting myself, I trip almost drown in pools of cottonwood leaves. I search for perfection only to find worm-eaten apples and frost nipped tomatoes. I catch a glimpse of myself in an acequia's leftover water, see choices desires flow in muddy patterns before my face. The seasons of my life pass before my eyes, my hands reach for something more than a watery reflection, while plastic once again covers my windows. Each cooling raindrop deepens my connection to spirit, and I offer up my experience for others to harvest, 'When I stumble I remember the 12 steps, and walk the seasons."

The wheel turns

Floating in Creator's hands, my reflection shimmers with willingness, safe at last in my center. I remember there is more than myself. I face the grandmothers all my relations, offer up myself, tobacco upon wind, corn meal to earth. I am the wheel. I walk with Spirit clearly my guide inside.

Changing the Story

Waves of addictions swirl in foamy water.
A storm screams,
my mouth opens,
wind swallows my shout,
blows me off course.

The shore, my core,
dribbles away with this tide,
that love,
this food,
that one drink
sure to fill the God-sized hole in my center.
Before I hit the edge, I surrender control of the storm inside.

Storms come and go,
compulsions dissolve,
I recover an ocean of self.
Seven seas hold the earth and my tears,
glacier melt overflows the banks
Earth changes and so do I.

I am, the Earth is, recovering,
growing more alive.
Truth, thunder rolls on,
rolls over my body crackles
with the electrical energy of genesis.
Rain devours earth, lightning sparks wind.
I am all elements spiraling together.

Earth's rage births hurricanes, tornados
purify the sun, sky and sea.
Salty storms break down my rage,
crushes my shell into a fresh sandy beach
I am the shore,
the rocks, my body.
I am the waves that crash against the shore,
the rocks,
my body.
I roar,
my body quakes in orgasmic rebirth.
I am, the earth is,
I am, the waves are,
swirling free of prison shells
great spiral tides of being.

Sticks and Stones

Modern Curses

I am called lady, smile sweetly, be nice, cross legs, tighten ass.
I am called hag, reek of cunty sweat, ragged clothes,
        persistently hairy.
I am called stupid, prattle softly, marry a man, do the expected.
I am called silly, giggle, cry easily, listen well, act vulnerable.
I am called bitch, know what's right, speak directly, stay specific.
I am called penis envy, assume a businesslike attitude, be assertive.
I am called invitation, eat a solo dinner, walk alone in a park.
I am called victim, encounter difficulties, live hurt, wish for mercy.
I am called mother, offer nurturance, give acceptance, remain loving.
I am called whore, howl in orgasm, fierce in heat, appear sexy
I am called witch, delight in thunderstorms, inspire as a catalyst.
I am called cow, give birth to sons, daughters, kiss tiny fingers.
I am called old lady, hold wisdom of years,
        bear gifts for generations.

Evergreen

thirteen women under a pregnant moon dance solemnly in a
        circle around a sacred fire.
a sweaty woman clad in a long flannel nightgown pads to the
        toilet to replace her bloody cloth.
two women press breast to breast slick fingers follow an internal
        rhythm, sighs swell faster and louder.
a panting woman crouches, pushes a crown through her cervix,
        one woman at each elbow watches intently.
a very small woman comforts her sad heart in the safe arms of a
        silver haired woman.
hundreds of women dance fiercely amongst the fir trees, their
fragile bodies' shields against the tumbling deaths of rooted sisters.
a silent rocking woman before her hearth dreams,
        cuddles a small black purr.
two women one prone the other leans over
        listens as secrets whisper,
release pain with breath, herbs steep friends with the fire.
one woman invokes a wrathful deity, sends forth her spirit's mirror.
five women sit share tea pass a talking stick,
        heal with gentle common words.
two small women and a larger guiding woman
        press sharply their shovels into moist brown earth
        turn over a richer blend, entices seeds.
one woman pedals faster as her hands coax wet grey clay,
        the birth of a useful vessel.
one woman lit by candlelight, many young and
        older women embrace her with their rapt attention,
        she emits bright sparks of words.

Ancient Mysteries

Call me Friend
I embrace you with
the gentleness of Deer

Call me Mother
I wash behind ears
massage small shoulders,

Call me Sister
I offer my open hand
gentle common words,

Call me Lover
I reflect
passions of your pure heart,

Call me Healer
I dance fiercely,
earthquakes, lightening

Call me Sappho
I love sisters,
mothers, bow to no man,

Call me Muse
I weave a siren call
to inspire action,

Call me Creatrix
I roll out fall into winter
with my breath,

Call me Dakini
I wear a garland of skulls
entrails in my teeth,

Call me Nightmare
I invade dreams
freeze genitals with fear,

Call me Earth
I give birth, bear heavy burdens,
die and go on,

Call me Goddess
I appear as mountains,
rivers flames, in every woman,

Call me Ocean
I contain
every precious tear shed,

Call me She Who
is Primordial Truth.

Lightning Strikes Twice

there is nothing delicate about lightning
or a cancer diagnosis
both seem to fall from the heavens
flash a sharp acrid smell,
rip apart the sky, our world
blind us
knock us senseless
then comes the thunderclap,
ricochets, reverberates, echoing
down to the core of our being.

once hit by lightning we never forget the smell,
the rush of adrenaline
or the lack of oxygen to our brains.

once hit by lightning we forget
our bodies are a hummingbird's kiss
frosty puffs of breath, a buffalo standing in the snow

once hit by lightning we must remember
the sentinel apple tree charred by a bolt
still sprouts new life, grows sweet fruit

there is nothing delicate about lightning
or red zippers of cancer scars
both are heaven's clarion call for fierce grace
welcome angels sow miracles while
we rest in the palm of God's hand.
We must whisper a wish to a butterfly

gaze at a little girl dancing with a firefly
become a shadow which runs across the grass
lose itself in the sunset
yet greet the roll of thunder come again.

Author's Bio

Laurel Thatcher Ulrich, "Well behaved women rarely make history." Mari Selby has always been an unruly woman. Mari's unruly behavior began as a child standing up to her bullying father, continued with her years of protesting the Vietnam War, and living communally with women in Oregon. Mari currently writes as a spiritual warrior and cultural subversive. Mari's first poem was written and published when she was seven.

In addition to *Lightning Strikes Twice*, Mari is currently working on an anthology; *Awaking the Hero Within: Stories from the Cancer Tribe*. Over decades Mari has published her poetry in anthologies, almanacs, magazines and newsletters. She has also taught and led writing groups and workshops. Today, Mari is a contributing writer for the "San Francisco Book Review" column, "After the Manuscript", and "Master Heart" magazine.

In a series of anthologies, Of Sticks and Stones Press will be expanding to include women's stories of transformation and courage.

For over three decades Mari has comforted and assisted hundreds of people as a family therapist, astrologer, hospice worker, healer, and spiritual advisor. For the past 14 years Mari has been the director of Selby Ink, a publicity and marketing firm.

Selby Ink promotes authors who make a difference by helping those authors to develop name recognition through social media and traditional publicity efforts. Selby ink specializes in the following genres: body-mind-spirit, relationships, environmental issues, and social justice. You can also find Mari on Facebook, or Twitter @selbyink.

www.SelbyInk.com
www.Lightning-Strikes-Twice.com

Artist's Bio

Jennet Inglis has exhibited and educated nationally and internationally for over two decades. Her paintings, drawings and sculptures are found in some of the finest private collections in Europe, Asia, and the United States. Jennet has won awards for her artwork; as well, her work has served to benefit numerous institutions, foundations, and organizations.

Jennet's passionate and rigorous study of science and nature evolved from an early age, as did her classical training in art. At the age of 13, Jennet attended her first adult Life-Drawing seminar. A few months later she enrolled in an undergraduate level course in geology at the American Museum of Natural History in New York City. Always a storyteller, Jennet has lectured in museums and cultural centers in Europe and America. Attendees of her programs often become colleagues and passionate collectors of her artwork. Trained in both science and art, Jennet is developing several book projects for ages eight to adult that are scheduled for publication in the very near future

You can view Jennet's artwork on FaceBook at Inglis Art, and at http://dakiniruleembodiment.shutterfly.com

   Post Office Box 791
   Staunton, VA. 24402
   ptdthunder2@yahoo.com
   mobile: 540 480 0868

https://www.facebook.com/pages/Inglis-Art/173051949454405?ref=ts&fref=ts

Book Order Form

Want to share this good news with a loved one or friend? Do you know other women who would be inspired by, empowered through or just plain love this poetry book?

There are 3 ways to order your copy of
Lighting Strikes Twice by Mari Selby

1. Order directly from the publication.
   Of Sticks and Stones Press
   by telephone 540-446-5573

2. On Amazon.com

3. Or by mailing the form below to:
   Of Sicks and Stones Press
   POB 791
   Staunton, VA 24402

Please send the number of copies of
Lighting Strikes Twice
as indicated on the form below to:

Name _____

Address _____

City _____ State_____ Zip_____

My personal check is enclosed for _____ # of copies
*First copy: $10.95 [plus $6.00 shipping & handling]

www.Lightning-Strikes-Twice.com

www.ingramcontent.com/pod-product-compliance
Lightning Source LLC
Chambersburg PA
CBHW071326040426
42444CB00009B/2091